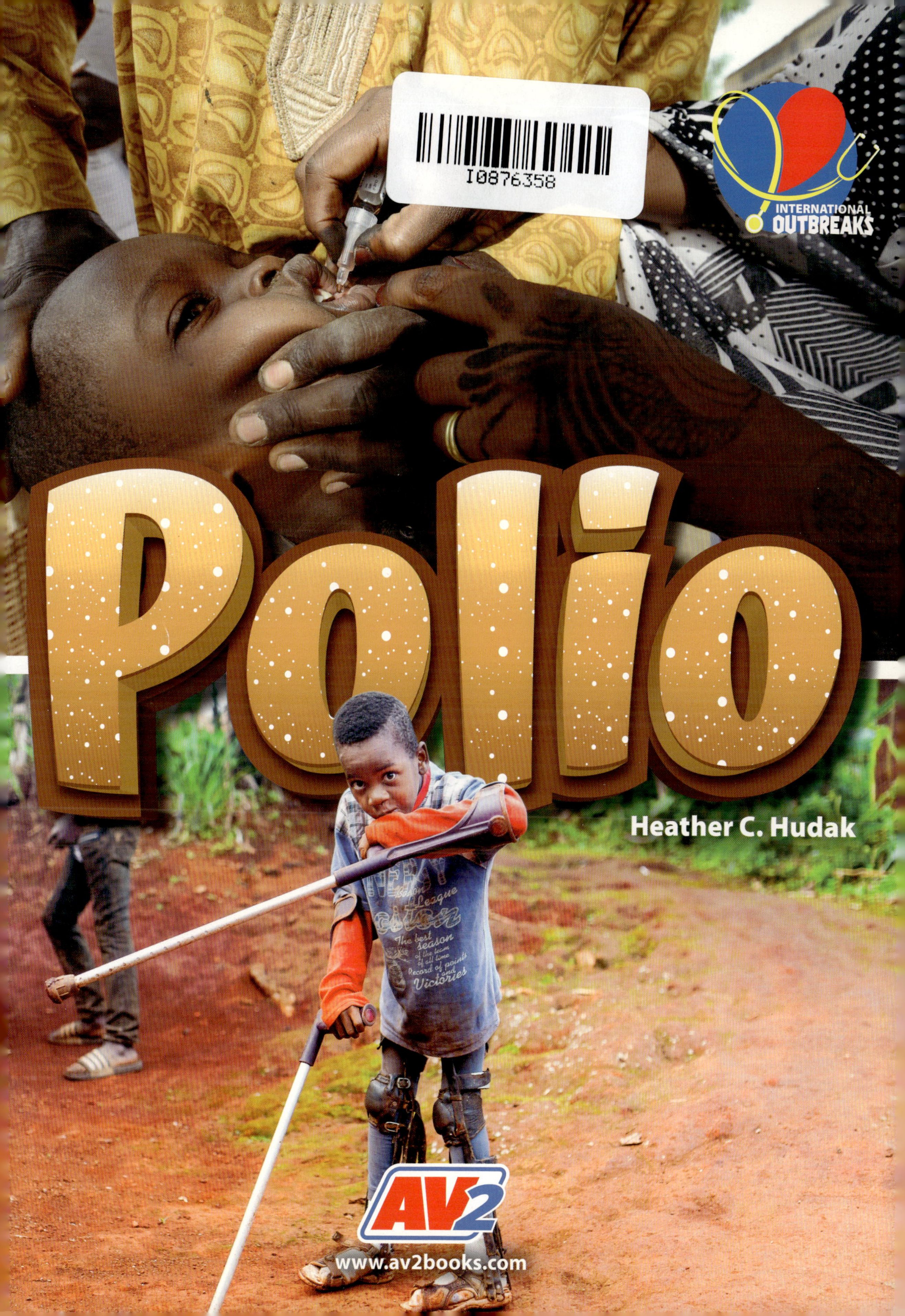

INTERNATIONAL OUTBREAKS

Polio

Heather C. Hudak

AV2
www.av2books.com

Step 1
Go to **www.av2books.com**

Step 2
Enter this unique code
NLPWS1K7S

Step 3
Explore your interactive eBook!

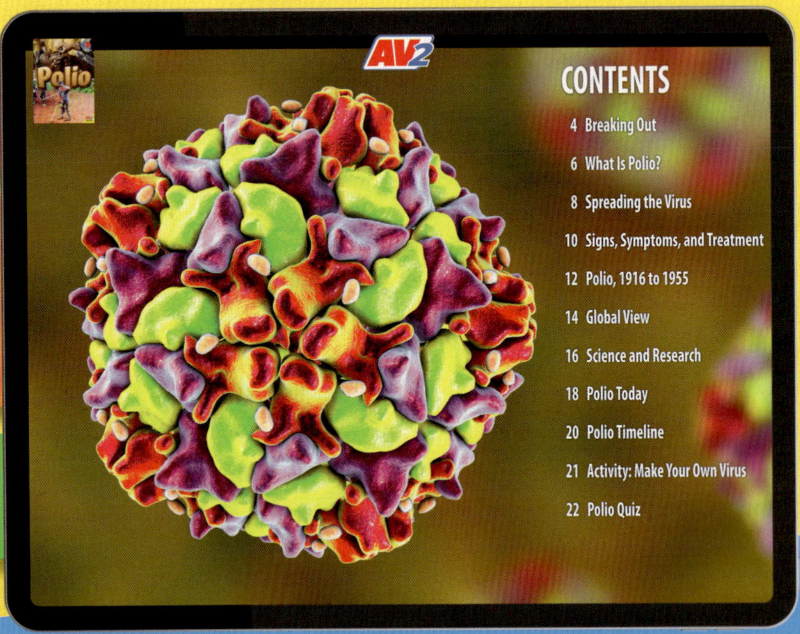

AV2 is optimized for use on any device

Your interactive eBook comes with...

Contents
Browse a live contents page to easily navigate through resources

Audio
Listen to sections of the book read aloud

Videos
Watch informative video clips

Weblinks
Gain additional information for research

Try This!
Complete activities and hands-on experiments

Key Words
Study vocabulary, and complete a matching word activity

Quizzes
Test your knowledge

Slideshows
View images and captions

... and much, much more!

INTERNATIONAL OUTBREAKS

Polio

CONTENTS

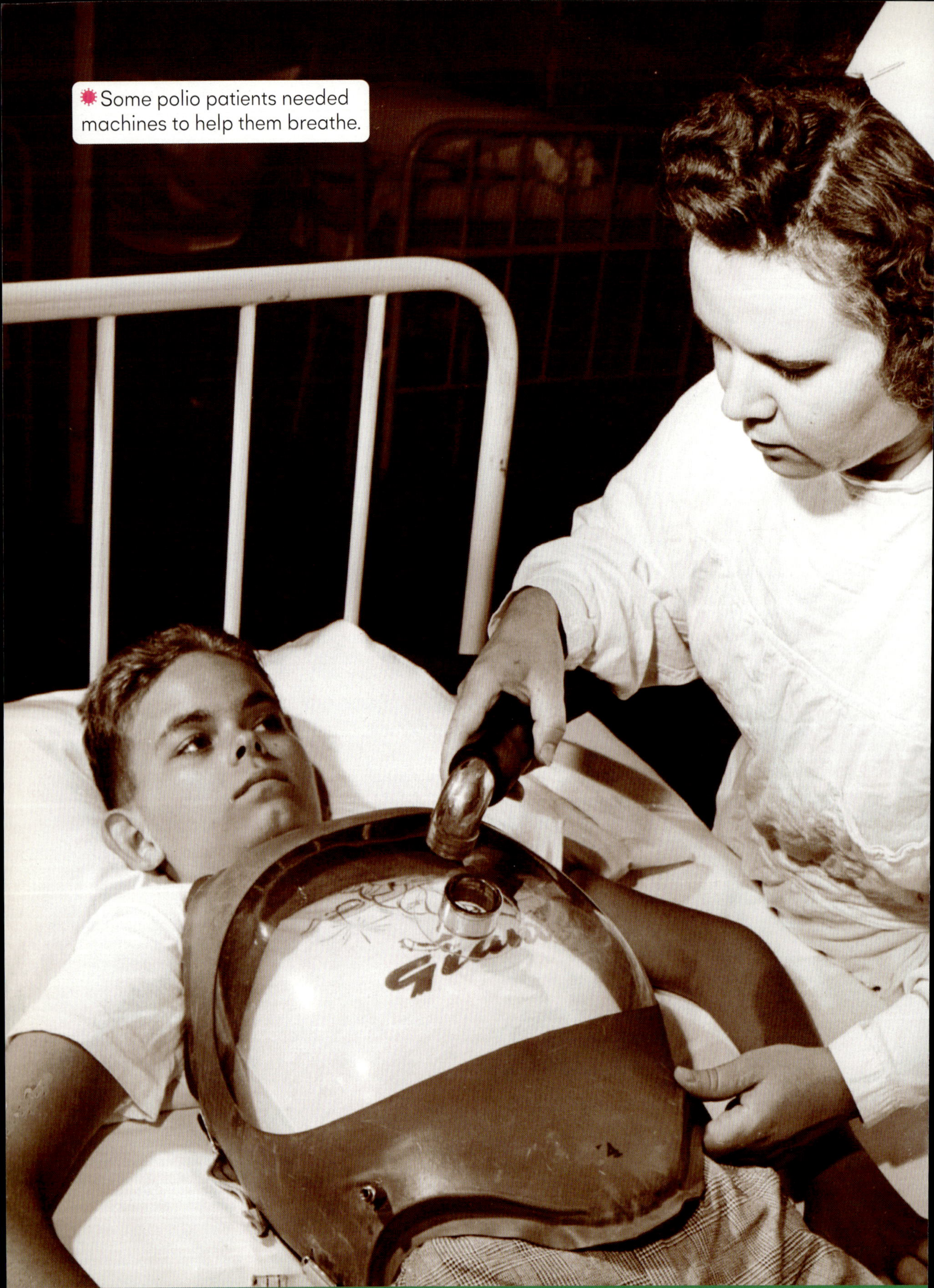

Some polio patients needed machines to help them breathe.

Breaking Out

Viruses are very tiny germs. They live in every kind of environment. Viruses cause many different **diseases**. Scientists are always trying to learn more about viruses. They look for ways to stop viruses from spreading and making people sick.

Scientists compare the number of diseases that happen from one year to the next. This tells them how many cases are normal for a certain time and place. Sometimes, there are more cases of a disease than usual. This is called an outbreak. It happens when a virus **infects** many people in the same place in a short time. An outbreak can last days, months, or even years. Doctors and health officials try to **contain** the virus. An epidemic happens when the virus spreads quickly to many people in a one area. The virus may even spread to a few different areas. There were many polio epidemics in the United States and around the world in the 1900s.

FAST FACT

The worst polio epidemic in the United States took place in 1952. There were 57,879 new cases that year alone. More than 3,100 people died, and over 20,000 people developed mild to severe **paralysis**.

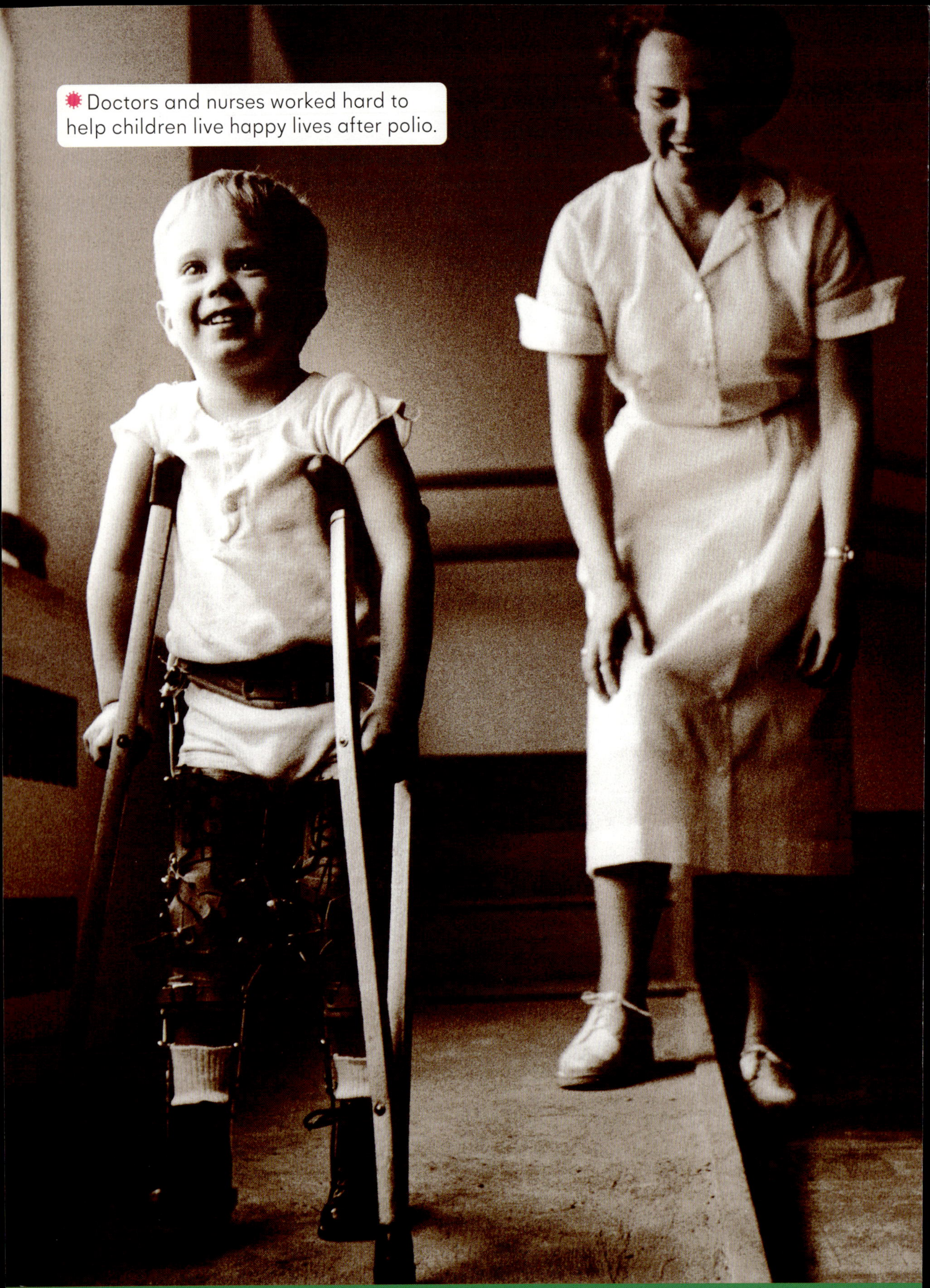

Doctors and nurses worked hard to help children live happy lives after polio.

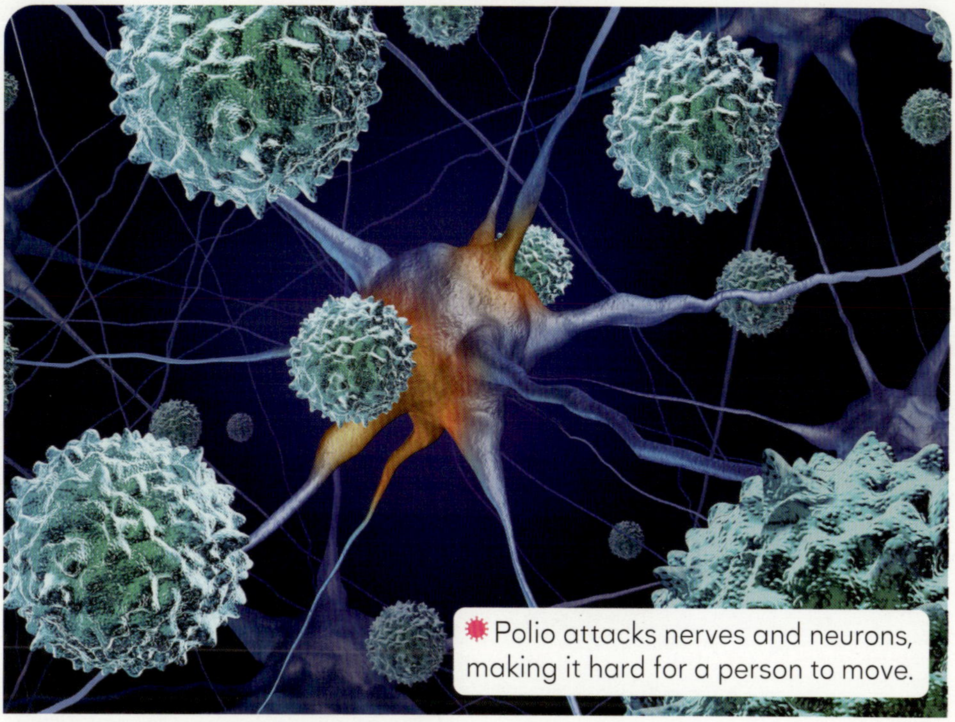

Polio attacks nerves and neurons, making it hard for a person to move.

What Is Polio?

Polio is short for poliomyelitis. It is an infectious disease caused by the poliovirus. Polio leads to only mild illness in most people. However, it can be life-**threatening**. Polio can infect a person's brain and spinal cord. It destroys the nerves that make muscles move. This can cause paralysis in a few cases. It can also lead to breathing problems and even death.

No one knows for sure where polio came from or when the first case took place. The disease has likely been around for thousands of years. Drawings from ancient Egypt show people with weak limbs using canes to help them walk. A doctor in the late 1700s talked about a disease that attacked the body from the hips to the toes. Experts believe it was polio. The first known polio outbreaks took place in Europe in the 1800s.

Contaminated water flows down the streets in some countries.

Spreading the Virus

Polio is very **contagious**. It spreads from person to person. The virus enters the body through the mouth and multiplies in the throat and intestines. It can make thousands of copies of itself in just a few hours. The virus then moves into the bloodstream and makes its way to the brain and spinal cord. It attacks the cells people need in order to swallow, breathe, and move their arms and legs. Polio only affects humans. Animals cannot get it.

Polio mainly spreads through contact with stool that comes from an infected person. People are most likely to get polio from drinking water that is contaminated with waste. This is especially true in poor countries that do not have proper toilets or sewage systems. Many developing countries do not have systems that clean their water. The water is therefore more likely to contain waste. In rare cases, polio can spread through droplets that come out when an infected person coughs or sneezes.

The poliovirus is too small to be seen without a special microscope.

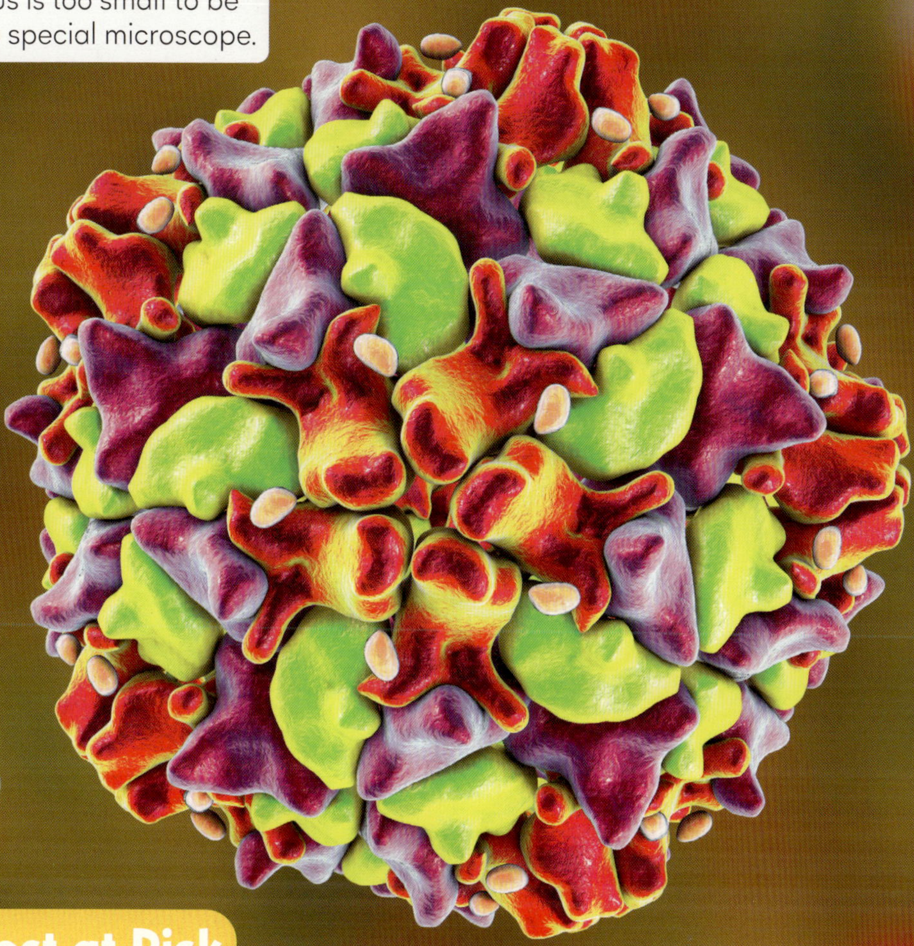

Most at Risk

Polio can infect anyone who has not been **immunized**, though some people have a greater chance of getting the virus. Polio mainly infects elderly people and children under the age of five. Pregnant women and people who have other diseases are also more likely to get polio. People who live with an infected person or work with the virus in a lab are at risk, too. Anyone who gets polio will not get the same type of poliovirus again.

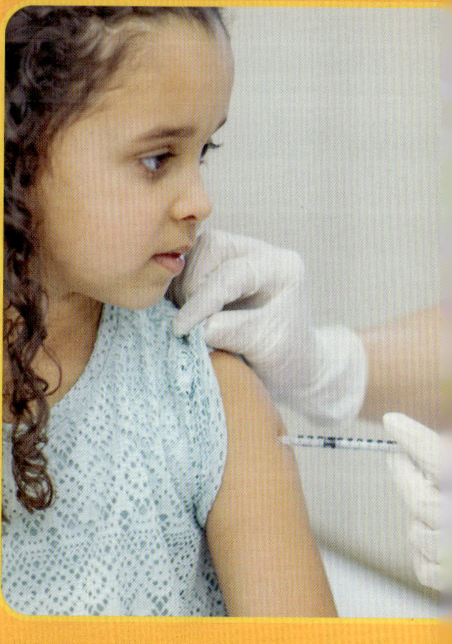

Signs, Symptoms, and Treatment

Most people who get polio never have any symptoms at all. About 5 to 10 percent have mild symptoms. People begin to show signs of the virus 7 to 17 days after they get it. A sore throat and fever are common polio symptoms. People may also feel sick and tired. Some may have a headache or stomach pain. The symptoms last for about two to five days. They usually go away on their own.

In rare cases, polio attacks the brain and spinal cord. People may feel pain in their back, arms, and legs. Their muscles may feel tender. They may have a stiff neck. Most people **recover** from the disease, but not all do. About 1 in 200 people are paralyzed by polio. Most people who are paralyzed by polio cannot move their arms or legs. Some cannot hold up their heads. Their mouths and eyelids droop. They may not be able to swallow or talk. About 5 to 10 percent of people who are paralyzed die because they cannot breathe well.

FAST FACT

Franklin Delano Roosevelt got polio in 1921. He was 39 years old. Roosevelt went on to become the president of the United States in 1933.

Polio can cause deformities of the limbs.

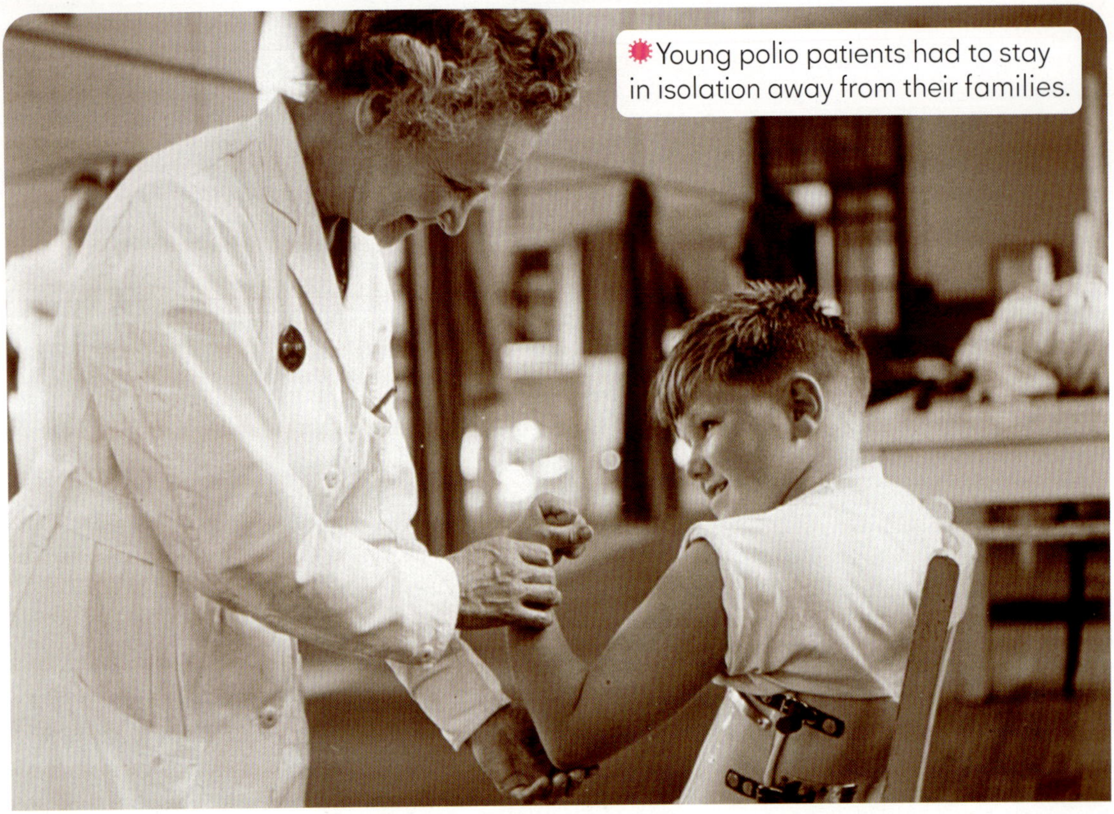

Young polio patients had to stay in isolation away from their families.

Polio, 1916 to 1955

The first known polio epidemic in the United States took place in Vermont in 1894. There were 132 cases and 18 deaths. A second polio epidemic struck New York in 1916. More than 9,000 people got the virus, and 2,300 died. Most of them were children. Schools closed. Businesses shut down. People hung signs on houses if someone inside had the virus. Sick children were taken from their families and sent to special hospitals away from others.

There were more than 27,000 cases across the country during the 1916 polio epidemic. People were terrified that they might get the disease. At the time, no one knew how it spread. The 1916 epidemic was the first of many over the next 40 years. The worst epidemic took place in 1952. There were 57,628 new cases that year alone.

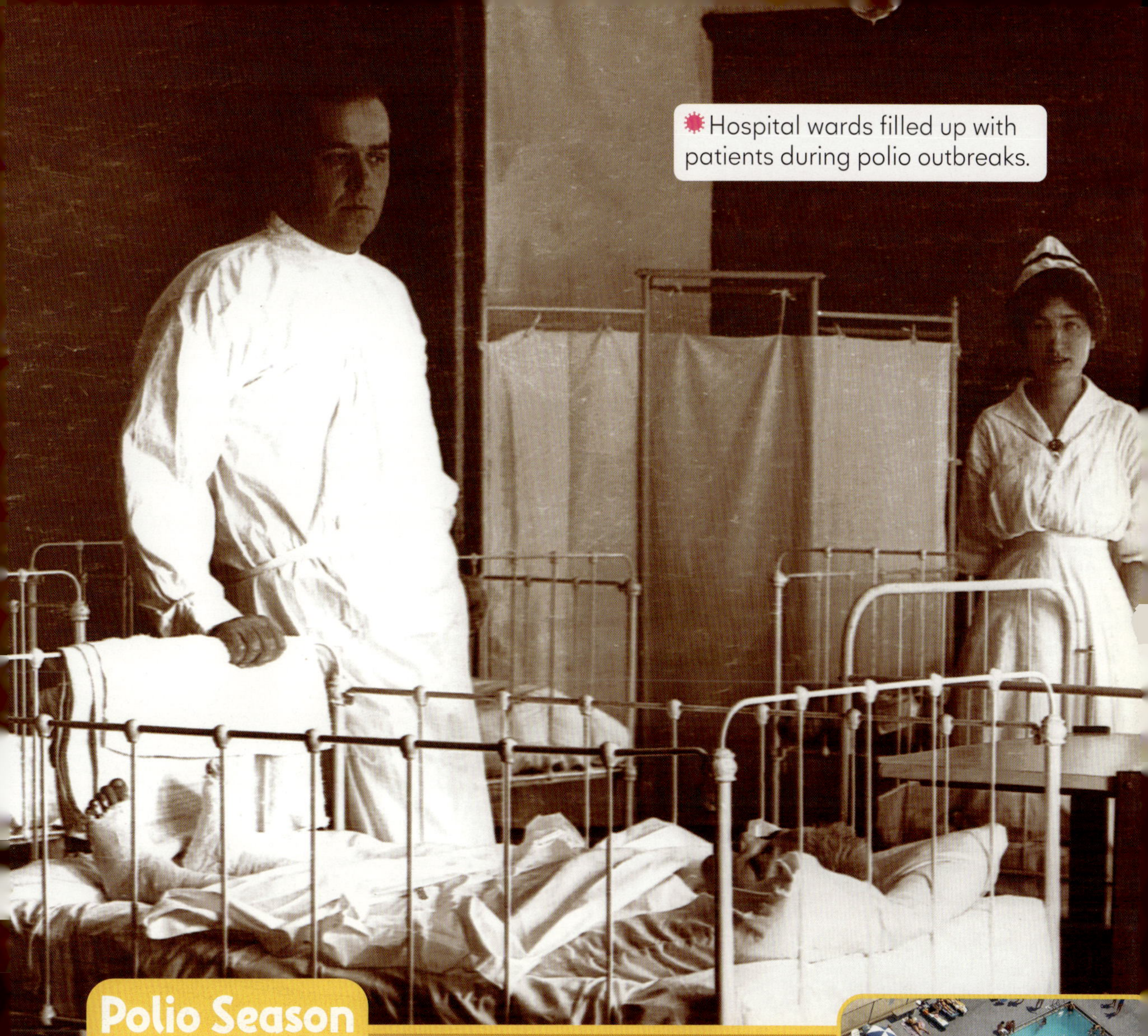

Hospital wards filled up with patients during polio outbreaks.

Polio Season

Polio outbreaks became worse during summer each year. July to September was known as polio season. Movie theaters asked people to sit far apart. Swimming pools, amusement parks, and other crowded places where children gathered closed down. People hoped this would help stop the virus from spreading. Hospitals put strict rules in place for treating the sick. Parents were urged to stay away from their children at home. People thought the disease could spread through kissing, sneezing, or coughing.

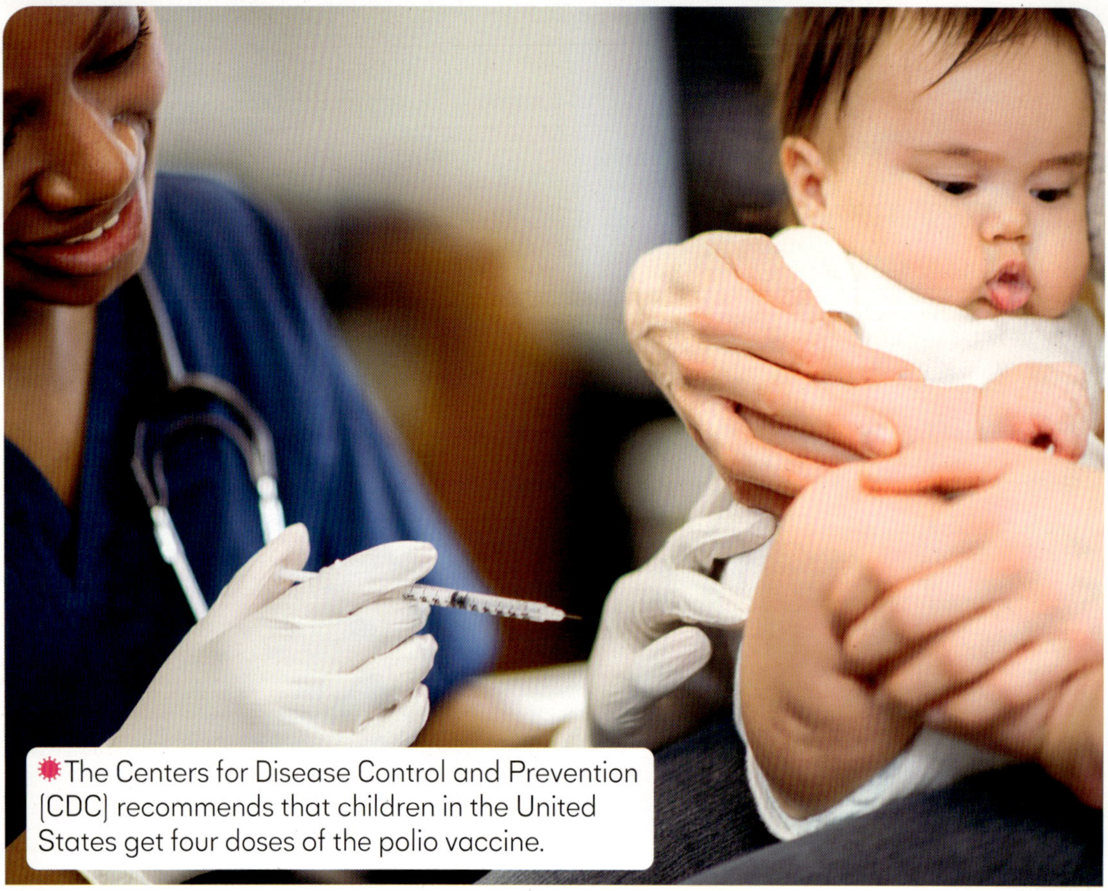

The Centers for Disease Control and Prevention (CDC) recommends that children in the United States get four doses of the polio vaccine.

Global View

Polio outbreaks took place in many parts of the world during the 20th century. At first, polio was found mainly in Europe, North America, Australia, and other developed nations. The disease then spread to developing nations, too. It infected hundreds of thousands of people all over the world. Finally, a **vaccine** was released in 1955.

About 450 million doses of the polio vaccine were given out over the next four years. Polio was no longer a major problem in the United States and other developed nations. However, many developing nations remained badly afflicted. The **World Health Organization** (WHO) began to help countries in need get vaccines.

Mapping Polio in Africa and South Asia in 2017

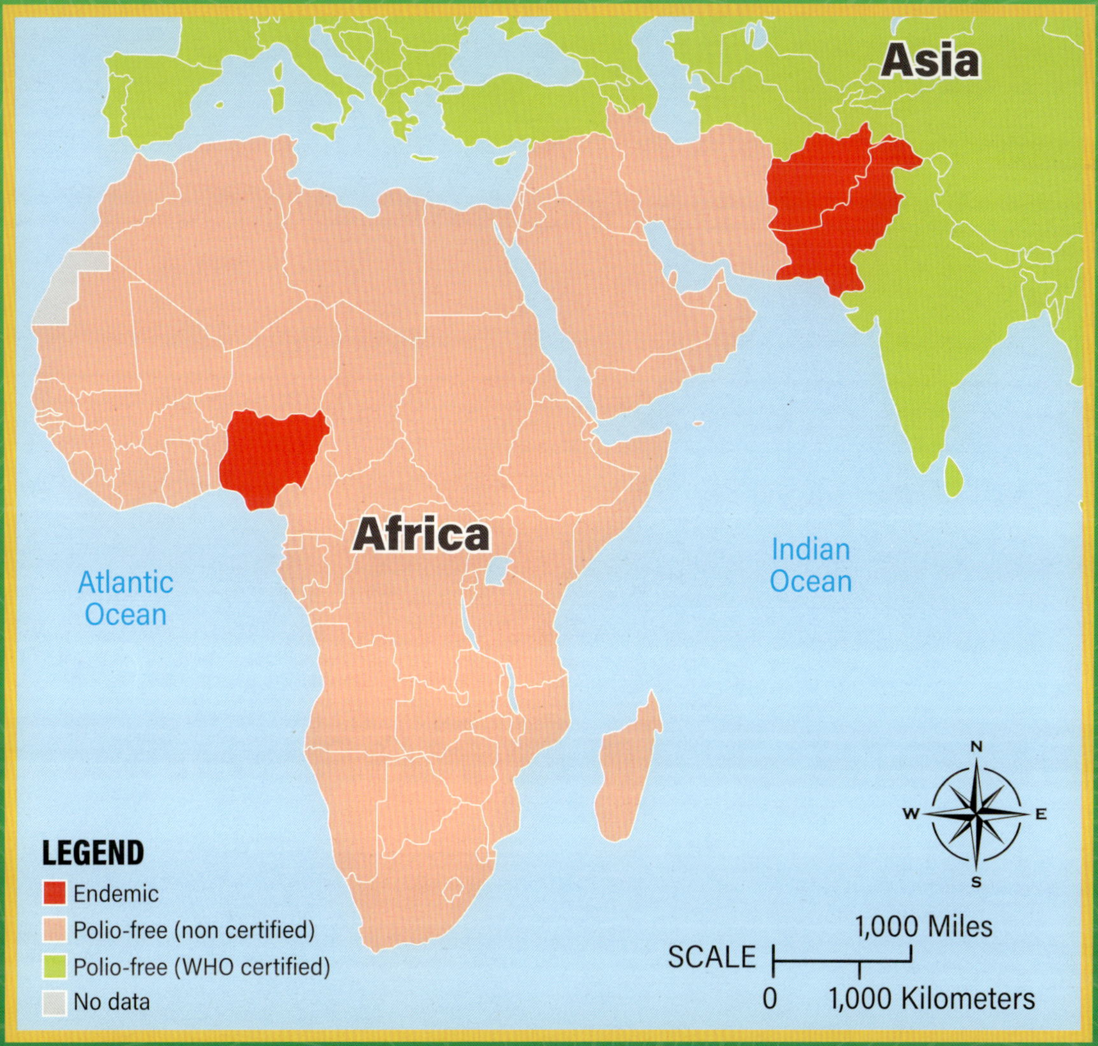

In **1988,** polio was found in **more than 125 countries.**

About **350,000 children were paralyzed** by polio each year prior to **1988.**

Today, the **number of polio cases is much lower.** There were **only 33 cases** reported in **2018.**

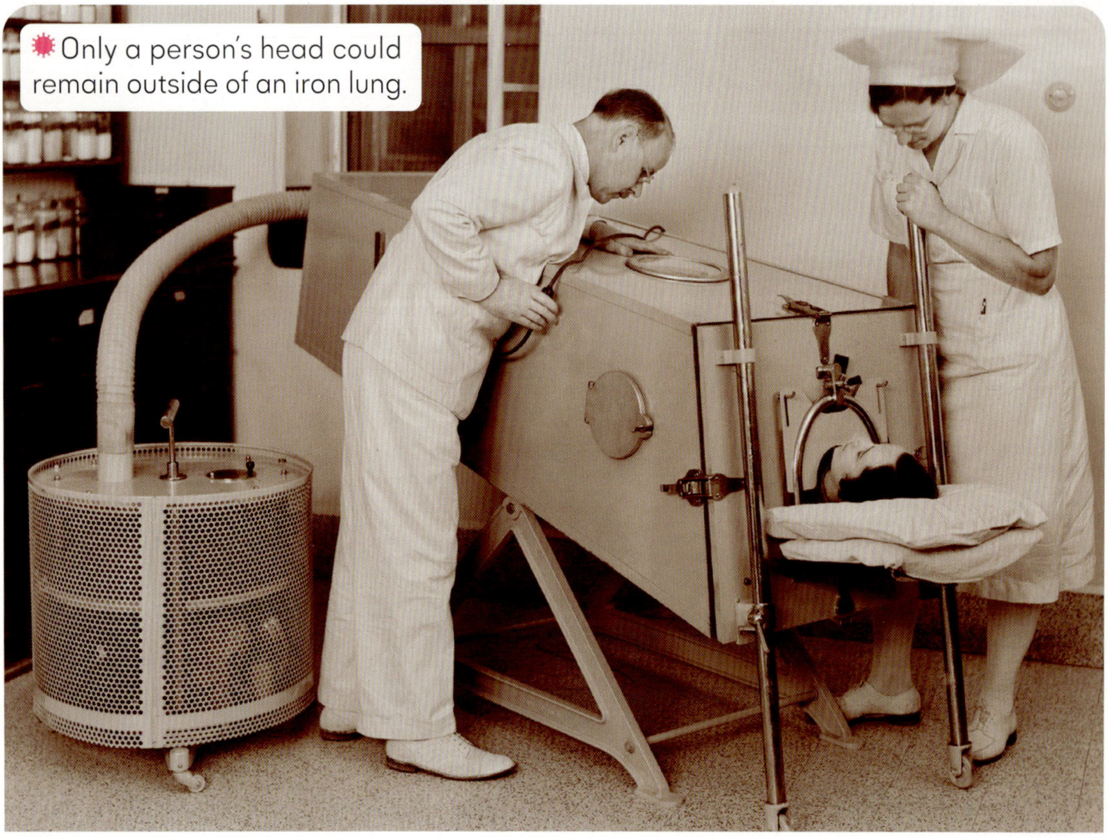

Only a person's head could remain outside of an iron lung.

Science and Research

Many people who were very sick with polio could not breathe well on their own. A device called an iron lung helped get air into their chests. It was invented in 1927. The sick person would lie on a bed inside a tank. Then, a pump would pull air in and out of the person's lungs. Hospitals set up special rooms with iron lungs.

In 1952, Dr. Jonas Salk developed a vaccine. It was tested on more than 1.8 million children in the spring of 1953. The vaccine worked. By 1955, the vaccine was ready to give to others. The number of U.S. polio cases fell from 35,000 in 1953 to 5,300 in 1957. A second vaccine came out in 1961. This vaccine, developed by Dr. Albert Sabin, has been used all over the world to stop the spread of polio.

Dr. Jonas Salk received grants from the National Foundation to create the polio vaccine.

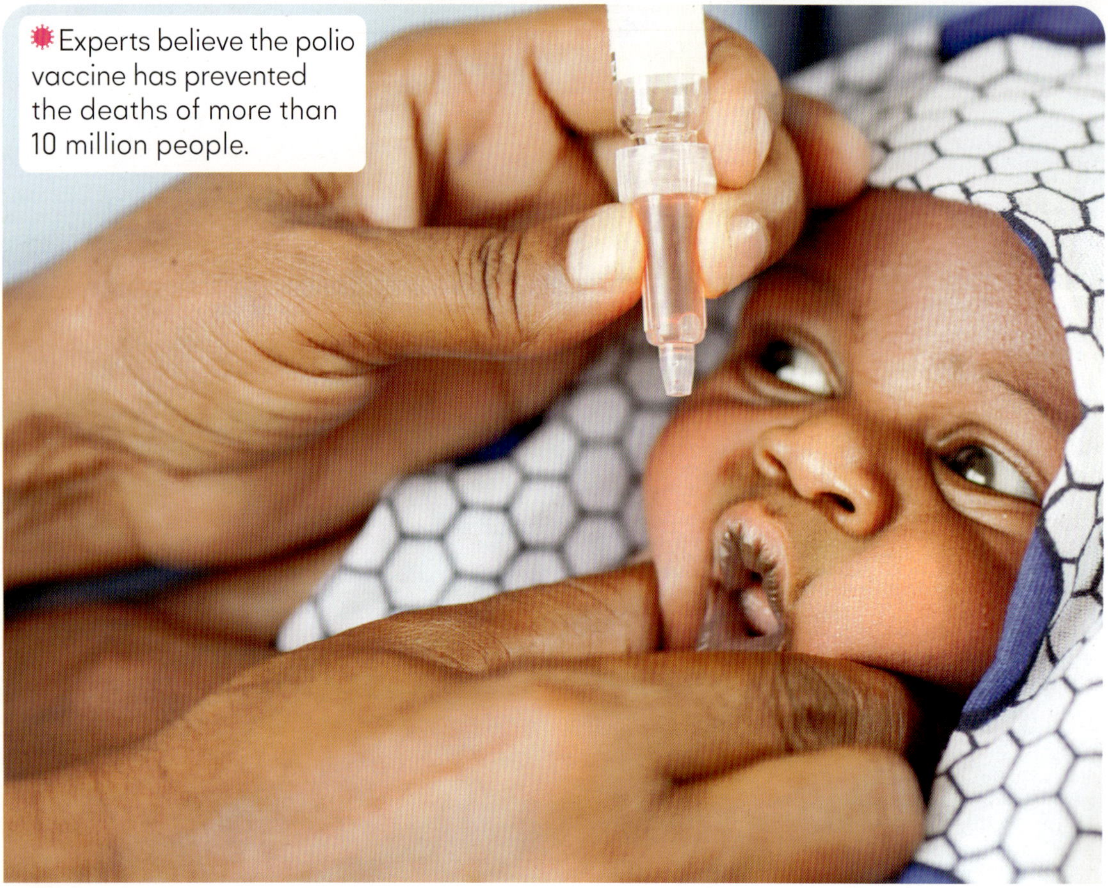

Experts believe the polio vaccine has prevented the deaths of more than 10 million people.

Polio Today

Today, polio is very rare. The virus is normally found in just two countries. They are Afghanistan and Pakistan. There are only a few dozen cases in these countries each year. However, there are small outbreaks in other countries, too. They mainly happen in developing countries in Africa and South Asia. These places do not have strong healthcare systems or the means to vaccinate everyone against the virus.

People who travel to countries infected with polio can bring the virus home with them. Even one case of polio can lead to many more. There is still no cure for polio. Immunization is the only way to stop the virus from spreading. The vaccine is given to children around the world.

Polio Immunization around the World between 1990 and 2018

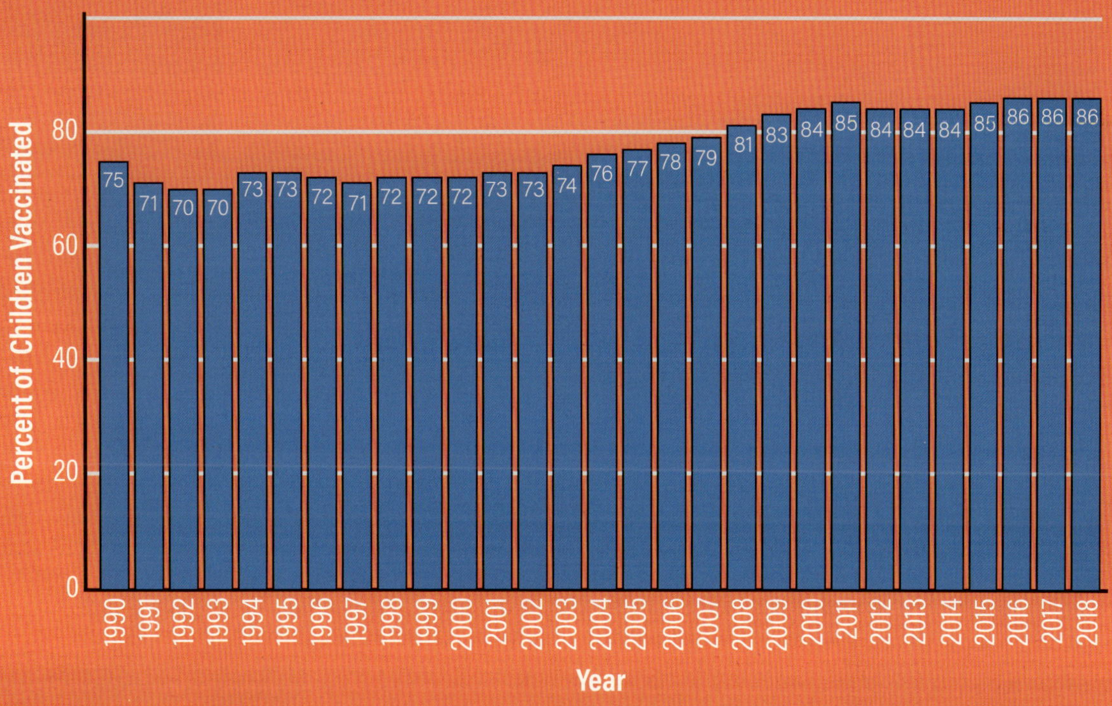

People lined up in long queues for the polio vaccine after it was made available.

Polio Timeline

1403–1365 BC
An Egyptian carving shows a man with a cane who seems to have polio.

1894 AD
The first polio epidemic in the United States takes place in Vermont.

1952
The number of polio cases reaches its peak in the United States. Dr. Jonas Salk develops a vaccine.

1955
Polio immunizations begin.

1961
A second polio vaccine is approved for use.

1988
Polio no longer exists in many countries, including the United States, the United Kingdom, and Australia. It remains in 125 other countries.

2020
Polio remains in just two countries, Afghanistan and Pakistan. Outbreaks still take place in some parts of the world.

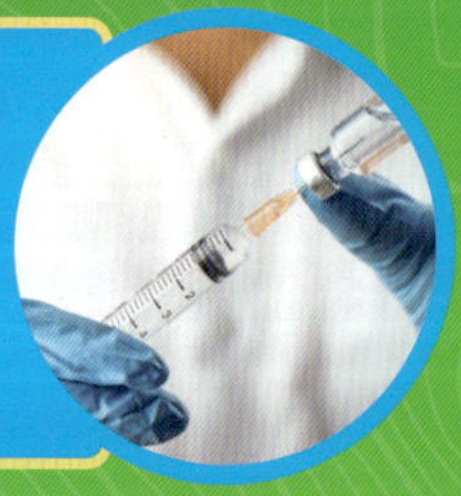

ACTIVITY
Make Your Own Virus

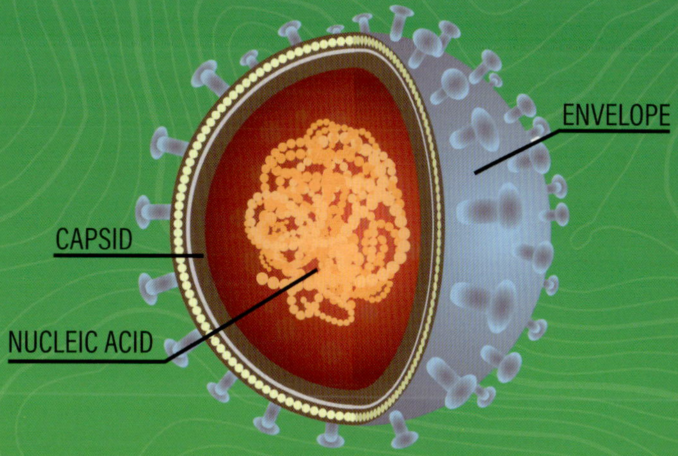

Have you ever wondered what a virus looks like? Viruses come in many different shapes and sizes. They have two main parts. First, they have nucleic acid. This is a set of instructions. Second, they have a protein coat called a capsid. It wraps around the nucleic acid like a shell. Some viruses have a third part called an envelope, which is made of fat and protein. Try this activity to make a virus of your own.

What You Need

- Pen
- Paper
- Crayons or colored pencils

What to Do

1. Come up with a name for your virus. Write the name at the top of the paper.
2. Then, think about what kind of disease your virus causes, and write it down, too. Be creative!
3. Write down the different symptoms of the disease.
4. How does your virus spread and who can get it? Write down those details next.
5. Draw a picture of what your virus looks like. Be sure to label the main parts of the virus.

POLIO QUIZ

1
Who invented the first polio vaccine?

2
How does polio spread?

3
Where was the first polio epidemic in the United States?

4
Who can get polio?

5
How can people stop the spread of polio?

6
When was the worst polio epidemic in the United States?

7
What is an iron lung?

8
Which countries still have polio?

ANSWERS
1. Dr. Jonas Salk
2. Through contact with stool that comes from an infected person or through infected droplets
3. Vermont
4. Any human
5. Through immunization
6. 1952
7. A device that helps people breathe
8. Afghanistan and Pakistan

Key Words

contagious: moves easily from one person to another

contain: keep under control

diseases: illnesses that have certain signs and symptoms

immunized: made a living creature immune, or able to fight off a virus, by giving them a vaccine against the virus

infects: contaminates a person or object with a disease-causing germ

paralysis: the loss of movement or feeling in all or part of the body

recover: get back to normal after feeling unwell

threatening: something that is likely to cause damage or harm

vaccine: a substance made from a small amount of a disease-causing germ to help provide immunity against that germ

viruses: very small germs that get inside the body and spread

World Health Organization: an organization that sets health standards and guidelines that many countries follow

Index

Get the best of both worlds.

AV2 bridges the gap between print and digital.

The expandable resources toolbar enables quick access to content including **videos**, **audio**, **activities**, **weblinks**, **slideshows**, **quizzes**, and **key words**.

Animated videos make static images come alive.

Resource icons on each page help readers to further **explore key concepts**.

Published by AV2
14 Penn Plaza, 9th Floor
New York, NY 10122
Website: www.av2books.com

Library of Congress Control Number: 2020943911

ISBN 978-1-7911-3238-5 (hardcover)
ISBN 978-1-7911-3239-2 (softcover)
ISBN 978-1-7911-3240-8 (multi-user eBook)
ISBN 978-1-7911-3241-5 (single-user eBook)

Printed in Guangzhou, China
1 2 3 4 5 6 7 8 9 0 24 23 22 21 20

082020
101119

Art Director: Terry Paulhus Project Coordinator: Priyanka Das

Every reasonable effort has been made to trace ownership and to obtain permission to reprint copyright material. The publisher would be pleased to have any errors or omissions brought to its attention so that they may be corrected in subsequent printings.

The publisher acknowledges Getty Images, iStock, Shutterstock, and Wikimedia as its primary image suppliers for this title.